Interviewing
More Than A Gut Feeling

Richard S. Deems, Ph.D.

American Media Publishing

4900 University Avenue
West Des Moines, IA 50266-6769
1-800-262-2557

Interviewing: More Than A Gut Feeling

Richard S. Deems, Ph.D.
Copyright ©1994 by American Media Inc.

This publication is designed to provide accurate and authoritative information in regard to the subject matter covered. It is sold with the understanding that neither the author nor the publisher is engaged in rendering legal, accounting, or other professional service. If legal advice or other expert assistance is required, the services of a competent professional person should be sought.

Credits:

American Media Publishing:	Arthur Bauer
	Todd McDonald
Editor:	Dave Kirchner
Designer:	Janet Ferguson Dooley
Project Manager:	Leigh Lewis

Published by American Media Inc., 4900 University Avenue, West Des Moines, IA 50266-6769

Library of Congress Catalog Card Number 94-70864
Deems, Richard S.
Interviewing: More Than a Gut Feeling

Printed in the United States of America
ISBN 1-884926-22-3

Foreword

For the past 20 years, I have coached job candidates on the interviewing process. I constantly listen as supervisors, managers, recruiters, and executive-search professionals talk about how they interview and the kinds of questions they ask. I listen to people in job-search situations describe the kinds of interviews they've experienced. Information from all of these sources has helped me successfully coach JobGetters.

When American Media Publishing approached me about writing this book, it didn't take me long to say, "yes." ***Interviewing: More Than a Gut Feeling*** has given me an opportunity to take what I have learned and apply it to the other side of the table—that of the interviewer.

If you've ever worried about...

- How to be more effective when you conduct a hiring interview
- How to predict a candidate's future job performance
- How to hire people who will truly be successful in their jobs

...then this book is for you. It will take you through the process of planning and conducting effective hiring interviews, and tell you how to evaluate the candidates to arrive at the right hiring decision.

There are two phrases you will read again and again throughout this book. The first is ***"The single best predictor of future job performance is past job behavior."*** The second is ***"...so you can hire the person who will be successful in the job."***

When you start using these phrases in talking to candidates, to peers, to subordinates, and also to superiors, you set in motion a mind-set that has the potential to radically change your hiring procedures. The result?

- Others will notice that people in your department are able to get things done.
- Others will notice that people in your department enjoy working with you.
- Others will notice that people in your department really enjoy their work.
- Finally, your boss will notice that your employee turnover has been reduced.

And all of this happens because you've taken the time and effort to hire people who truly will be successful in their jobs.

Now, here's to your success!

Richard S. Deems, Ph.D.

How to Read This Book

This book has been designed to be highly user-friendly! The writing style is easy to understand, and the organization of each chapter is simple to follow. Interactive exercises in each chapter will help you think through the information you've read and make it your own. To help you even further in your understanding of this material, try these suggestions:

 Turn to the **Table of Contents** to see how the book is organized.

 Take a quick look through the book, scanning or reading headings and paragraphs that interest you. Try to get a feel for how the book is organized and what it has to say.

 Put the book down and write out three questions you have about interviewing—questions that may have prompted you to read this book in the first place.

 Review your first question and try to identify a key word, phrase, or topic that might indicate where in the book this question will be answered. Turn again to the **Table of Contents**, and look for that key word, phrase, or topic. If you don't find it there, think of another word or phrase that relates to your question.

 When you've found a reference in the **Table of Contents**, turn to the part of the book that deals with your question and look for the answer. If you are referred to other sections or chapters, read those additional pages, too. Continue until you have your answer.

 Use this same procedure for the rest of your questions. As you find answers to each of them, you may come up with still other questions. If you do, just repeat the process.

Of course, you also can pick up the book and begin reading from cover to cover. Each chapter begins with objectives and contains interactive exercises for you to complete.

Perhaps most important, an **Interview Planning Guide** is included to help you prepare for your interviews.

The publisher and the author hope that our information truly helps you in your efforts to hire the right person for your job...based on *more than a gut feeling*.

About the Author

Richard S. Deems, Ph.D., is the founder and CEO of Deems Associates Inc, a national career-management consulting firm. For nearly 20 years, Dr. Deems has helped thousands of people across this country and in Canada prepare to interview for jobs with confidence.

In ***Interviewing: More Than a Gut Feeling***, Deems presents a step-by-step system to help decision-makers implement effective hiring decisions—decisions based on ***more than a gut feeling.***

Deems received his bachelor's degree from Nebraska Wesleyan University, his master's degree from Northwestern University, and his Ph.D. from the University of Nebraska at Lincoln, with an emphasis in adult development.

He is the author of numerous articles on career-management issues, and is frequently quoted as an expert in the career-management field. Deems is also the author of *I Have To Fire Someone!,* from American Media Publishing.

Table of Contents

Chapter Six

How Do I Evaluate and Select? 64

Chapter Seven

How Do I Handle Difficult Interviewing Situations? 76

Chapter Eight

How Do I Implement Behavior-Based Interviewing? 84

Appendices

Why "More Than A Gut Feeling"?

Chapter Objectives:

After reading this chapter and completing the interactive exercises, you should be able to understand:

- Why hiring needs to be based on **more than a gut feeling**.

- How past behavior is the single best predictor of future performance.

- Your company's true costs for employee turnover.

- The dangers of litigation due to faulty hiring practices.

- How hiring practices affect the company's reputation.

- The hiring process.

A lot of hiring gets done based on **nothing other than a gut feeling**. Assumptions. Intuition.

And a lot of employee turnover results because that gut feeling, that assumption, that intuition, just wasn't very accurate. The person who seemed so perfect in the interview couldn't get the job done. That person with the pleasant personality really didn't have the job skills you needed. The candidate who had a fast answer for every question during the interview couldn't take the fast pace on the job.

If you're like most managers, one of your greatest fears is that you'll hire the wrong person. You want to hire the person who, ultimately, will be the most successful in the job. That's because you know from experience that your operation will function more smoothly and will be more productive if the right person is in the right job.

If you're like most managers, your greatest need is for a system of interviewing that doesn't force you to rely on a gut feeling or your intuition. You want a system that enables you to gather the right information and use it to make informed hiring decisions. You want a system that has built-in predictability, so you know that the person you hire will be successful on the job.

This book will introduce you to the practice of behavior-based interviewing. The concept of behavior-based interviewing is simple: Your interview questions target the candidate's past job behavior...because past behavior is a reliable predictor of future performance.

Past Behavior Predicts Future Performance

The single best predictor of a candidate's future job performance is his or her past job behavior. How do we know this is true? Because it's been proved in thousands of actual job situations for more than two decades. Interviews that probe for past job behavior have been found to be more reliable than ones that focus on personality traits, such as "I'm dependable," or "I'm hardworking," or even, "You can count on me." And hiring decisions based on actual behavior are far more accurate than those based on gut feelings.

"The best single predictor of a candidate's future job performance is his or her past job behavior."

What many successful interviewers have found is that the way in which a person handled a specific situation in the past gives you valid information about how that person will approach a similar situation in the future. If a person has worked well with customers in the past, he or she most likely will be effective with customers in the future. If the person has had trouble communicating well in the past, you can predict that he or she will continue to have communication problems in the future.

This is the foundation for behavior-based interviewing. Once you understand this concept, you can plan to ask the kinds of questions that will give you the information you need to make good hiring decisions.

Employee Turnover

Employee turnover costs money, and the cost typically is a lot higher than most managers think it is. The cost of turnover includes everything from recruiting costs, the time to screen and interview new candidates, and the time and money to train the new employee...to the cost of lost work on the job while all this is taking place. In some positions, lost work translates into lost business, because customers or potential customers go somewhere else while the new employee is on the learning curve of effectively performing the job.

Some companies have identified employee-turnover costs as ranging from 35 percent to as much as 100 percent of the employee's annual salary. One organization estimated that it cost them in excess of $10 million annually to recruit, hire, and train more than 500 new manager-trainees. Bottom line: Employee turnover—for whatever reason—is extremely costly!

Obviously, you can't hope to eliminate employee turnover completely; it's a fact of modern business life that people change jobs. But you can reduce needless employee turnover—by doing all you can to make certain you hire the right person in the first place.

"Employee turnover costs money."

10

Take a Moment...

Stop for a moment and do your own analysis of the real cost of employee turnover. Think of a recent situation in which you had to replace someone because the original hiring decision was a poor decision. Now review the items listed below and assign a dollar cost to each item. You will need to estimate many of these costs, but try to be realistic. Add them up and you'll have a good idea of the total cost of just one instance of employee turnover.

$_____ Lost productivity while the position is vacant

$_____ Recruiting costs: advertising and/or agency fees

$_____ Screening costs: reviewing resumes, responding to inquiries, and providing information about the job

$_____ Interviewing costs: time spent contacting candidates, arranging interviews, preparing for each interview, and conducting the interviews

$_____ Evaluating costs: time spent evaluating the candidates and making the selection

$_____ The cost of making the job offer: time spent negotiating with the successful candidate and arranging the start date

$_____ Training costs: the money and cost of introducing the new employee and training him or her

$_____ The cost of reduced efficiency as the new employee learns the job

$_____ Other employee-turnover costs that you have identified

$_____ **Total Cost of One Instance of Employee Turnover**

Exposure to Litigation

Federal legislation mandates that companies practice nondiscriminatory actions during the hiring process. This means that, by law, you are not allowed to make your hiring decisions based on anything other than bona fide occupational qualifications. In other words, if a person has the necessary skills to be successful in the job, you cannot discriminate based on:

- Age
- Sex
- Ethnic origin
- Religious preference or affiliation
- Sexual preference
- Marital status
- Disabilities

This also means that you can't ask certain kinds of questions during the hiring interview, or list them on any application forms. Chapter Four – "How Can I Develop Fair and Effective Questions?" – will help you clarify what is and what is not discriminatory.

As our culture becomes more diverse, there has been an upsurge in the number of complaints filed about discriminatory hiring practices. Though a charge of discrimination often is difficult to prove, it also can be very difficult and costly to defend.

Marketplace Response

The public forms opinions of companies. One thing people always discuss when they talk about an organization is how good (or poor) a job it does in hiring. When an organization earns a reputation for excellence in hiring, invariably it also enjoys a good reputation in the marketplace, and several things happen:

- The organization is able to attract top candidates.
- Productivity is high.

- Employees enjoy working for the organization.
- People are more prone to buy the organization's products and services.

You can help build a positive image for your organization each time you interview someone. And each successful impression you make often is followed by more success.

The Hiring Process

When you understand what really takes place in the hiring process, you'll understand why it's necessary to make hiring decisions based on *more than a gut feeling*. You will understand that you need to:

- Think through the skills needed to be successful on the job.
- Prepare questions that will get each candidate to talk about these needed skills.
- Go beyond your gut reactions or assumptions as to who is best qualified for the job.
- Understand the hiring process.

Identifying an Unmet Need

The hiring process (See diagram on page 14) begins with the identification of an unmet need. An unmet need may be a task that needs to be accomplished. Maybe it's a new need, or perhaps it exists because of a job vacancy. Just as a person sometimes must take inventory of his or her experience and best skills and abilities, it's important to assess the specific employee skills and abilities that will best answer this unmet need.

You need to translate your unmet need into a job description that lists the various duties, tasks, and responsibilities of the job. The more detailed the job description, the easier it will be for you and your candidates to understand exactly what kinds of skills and experience are necessary for success in the job.

"You can help build a positive image for your organization each time you interview someone."

Making a Match

The interview is the interaction between the decision-maker and the candidate that attempts to find out if the candidate has these necessary skills. When there is a match, there is a job offer.

Ultimately, the hiring process is successful only when the hiring decision is based on this match between required job skills and demonstrated candidate skills and experience...in other words, on *more than a gut feeling*.

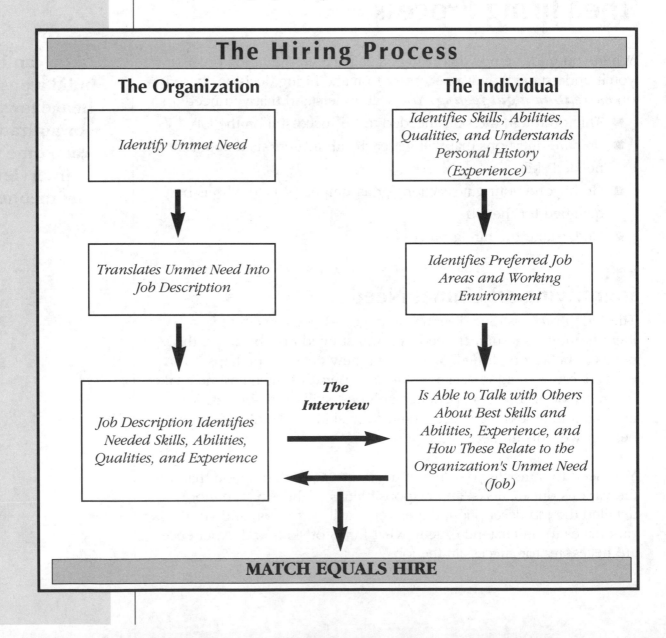

The Hiring Process

The Organization | **The Individual**

Identify Unmet Need

Identifies Skills, Abilities, Qualities, and Understands Personal History (Experience)

Translates Unmet Need Into Job Description

Identifies Preferred Job Areas and Working Environment

Job Description Identifies Needed Skills, Abilities, Qualities, and Experience

The Interview

Is Able to Talk with Others About Best Skills and Abilities, Experience, and How These Relate to the Organization's Unmet Need (Job)

MATCH EQUALS HIRE

Chapter One Review

Indicate **True or False** for each of the statements below. Suggested answers appear on page 89.

_____ 1. The single best predictor of future job performance is past job behavior.

_____ 2. Employee turnover can cost as much as 10 percent of the employee's salary.

_____ 3. Companies that are effective in hiring enjoy good reputations in the marketplace.

_____ 4. During the job interview, you cannot ask a candidate's age or ethnic origin.

_____ 5. During the job interview, you can ask about a candidate's marital status.

_____ 6. Companies that are thought to use discriminatory hiring practices often find it difficult to recruit top candidates.

_____ 7. A poor-performing employee can negatively affect the entire work unit.

_____ 8. Successful hiring involves a lot more than relying on just a gut feeling.

CHAPTER TWO

How Do I Identify the Needed Job Skills?

Chapter Objectives:

After reading this chapter and completing the interactive exercises, you should be able to:

 Identify and describe the technical skills needed for the job.

 Identify and describe the performance skills needed for the job.

Hiring the right person the first time takes *more than a gut feeling*. It takes planning and preparation, all of which begins with...

- Understanding the job and what it involves.
- Understanding the technical skills the job requires.
- Understanding the performance skills the job requires.
- Describing those skills in objective, behavioral terms.

The result? You will be able to interview and evaluate candidates in such a way that you get the information you need to identify the right person for the job.

Here's how to get started.

Understanding the Job

As a first step, take the time to review your understanding of the job for which you'll be interviewing. You can do this by reviewing existing job descriptions and evaluations of employees in the job. If there are other employees who hold similar positions, talk with them about what their jobs involve. Questions that will give you specific information to better understand the job include:

- Does the person manage others?

- Does the job involve making decisions relating to policy and/or procedures?

- What specific technical skills does the job involve?

- What specific performance skills does the job involve?

- Does the job involve direct contact with company customers?

- With what departments does the job relate?

- Is there anything else important about this position?

Even if you have had years of experience working with employees who hold this position, you will increase your awareness of just what it takes to be successful in that job by writing out your own understanding of the position and the skills it requires. This description need not be as lengthy as a full job description, but it does need to include whatever information will give you an in-depth understanding of what the job is about.

Job-description Statement Examples

Example 1:

This position involves supervising three others in the customer-service unit. The employee will need to make decisions and follow established guidelines on how to handle customer questions. The employee will need to use a Simplex Phone System in communicating with customers and staff, and a PC to enter data into our specialized program. The employee will be trained on decision-making guidelines as well as the computer software. After training, the employee will be expected to handle 80 percent of customer inquiries without assistance from peers or superiors.

Example 2:

This is an entry-level data-entry position in mortgage processing. The employee will be expected to enter data on a networked PC using our company's proprietary processing software, and will generate correspondence using Microsoft® Word for Windows 6.0. The only contact the employee will have with company customers is through correspondence. Performance goals will be established after a training period.

Example 3:

This position involves fabricating steel containers that will hold component-control mechanisms. The employee will need to read blueprints to identify the size and shape of the container, and where any special welds may be located. The employee will fabricate the container from lightweight steel panels and join the sides with several spot welds. Performance standards will be established, and bonus pay will be based on exceeding those performance standards.

When you can briefly describe the position and its requirements using these kinds of statements, you are ready to identify the technical skills needed for the job in greater detail.

Take a Moment...

Think of a position you need to fill in the near future. Using the provided examples as suggested formats, write your own brief job-description statement. As you continue with this chapter, you'll be asked to refer to this statement several times.

_____

_____

_____

_____

_____

_____

_____

_____

_____

_____

Identify the Technical Skills You Need for the Job

Your next task is to identify the technical skills you need for the job. Technical skills are those that call upon specific technical knowledge or experience, such as...

- Using specific kinds of machines.

- Using specific kinds of computer hardware and software.

- Manipulating tools in prescribed and precise ways.

Using *Example 1* on page 18, here are the technical skills that are required for the person to be successful on the job:

- PC skills: the ability to use a PC
- Data-entry skills using popular software programs
- A working knowledge of the Simplex Phone System

What Do You Really Need?

You will need to decide if previous experience is important for these technical skills, or if you will train the successful candidate. Though technical skills are often more easily learned than performance skills, many times jobs require that the employee begin with previous experience in one or more technical skills. Your review of the position will help you determine what's really needed. Once you identify the technical skills, you can focus on the performance skills the job requires.

Take a Moment...

Using the job-description statement you prepared on page 19, identify the specific technical skills the employee must have to be successful.

_____

_____

_____

_____

_____

Identify the Performance Skills You Need for the Job

Performance skills are the tasks and responsibilities assigned to the position that may relate to:

- Managing other employees.

- Making and being responsible for decisions.

- Following established guidelines.

- Following policies and procedures.

- Dealing with other departments.

- Dealing with the public.

- Receiving an assignment and reporting its results when completed.

Performance skills are closely tied to work habits that reflect the way a person gets a job done.

Using *Example 1* from page 18, here is a list of performance skills required for the job:

- Supervise three customer-service representatives (CSRs).

- Follow established guidelines.

- Apply established guidelines to specific customer inquiries.

- Help CSRs apply established guidelines to specific customer inquiries.

- Present information to CSRs and customers.

- Interact with other departments as needed.

- Cope with the pressure of numerous simultaneous inquiries.

- Solve work-unit problems.

2

Take a Moment...

Again, using the job-description statement you wrote earlier on page 19, list the performance skills the employee must have to be successful in that job. You may want to ask a human-resources specialist familiar with recruiting and selection to work with you, as well.

_____

_____

_____

_____

_____

_____

Prepare Your Questions

The time to prepare your questions is before the job interview. But before you can do this, you need to:

1. *Familiarize* yourself with the position.

2. *Identify* the technical and performance skills needed to be successful on the job.

3. *Match* the words you use to describe the job with the job skills needed to be successful in it.

Preparing the right questions takes time. It also requires an understanding of the different kinds of questions you can ask, and which ones will give you the information you need. These important interviewing skills are covered in Chapter Three, "How Do I Prepare My Questions?"

Chapter Two Review

Please answer the two questions below. Suggested answers appear on page 89.

1. Here is a brief position description. From this description, identify at least four technical skills and at least seven performance skills needed to be successful in this job:

    This position supervises five programmers who provide accounting assistance to three departments. The person in this position will identify the priority of specific projects and assign staff to work on each of them. The person will need to be familiar with the COBOL and BASIC programming languages, and able to help people in end-user departments use Lotus 1-2-3, Q&A, and proprietary software programs. In addition, the person will need to be familiar with networked PCs and be able to recommend appropriate PC software for departmental use, specifically in the marketing, sales, and marketing research departments.

Technical Skills

1. _____
2. _____
3. _____
4. _____

Performance Skills

1. _____
2. _____
3. _____
4. _____
5. _____
6. _____
7. _____

How Do I Prepare My Questions?

Chapter Objectives:

After reading this chapter and completing the interactive exercises, you should be able to:

 Describe three basic guidelines for developing questions.

 Prepare rapport-building questions and statements.

Prepare open-ended questions.

 Prepare probing questions for specific information.

Ask non-question questions.

Asking the right questions is your single best way to get the right kinds of information during the interview—the kinds of information that will lead you to the best hiring decision. Here's how to develop your questions so they'll give you the results you need.

> "Asking the right questions is your single best way to get the right kinds of information during the interview."

Guidelines for Developing Questions

Before you begin preparing your questions, take time to understand these three important guidelines.

 Avoid asking questions that can be answered by a single word, usually a simple "Yes" or "No." Single-word answers don't give you much information, and they don't give the candidate an opportunity to tell you all you need to know about that person. Examples of questions that don't provide you with much valid information include:

- *"Do you like working with people?"*
- *"Did you like your last job?"*
- *"Do you like working with PCs?"*

Instead of asking questions that can be answered with just a single word, you want to pose questions that invite the candidate to talk about what he or she has done in the past. As the candidate talks, you have an opportunity to get the information you need in order to make an informed hiring decision.

 Use open-ended questions that ask for specific examples of past job behavior. Remember, past behavior is the best indicator of future performance! This means asking focused questions that prompt the candidate to talk about past job experiences in very specific detail.

Instead of asking hypothetical questions about how the candidate might handle some future task, ask—specifically—how the candidate handled something similar in his or her past or present position. Since past behavior is the best indicator of future performance, you want to get the candidate talking about how the person handled situations similar to those that will be experienced in the new job. Keep your questions focused so the candidate doesn't ramble and provides the specific information you need.

"Past behavior is the best indicator of future performance!"

Keep your questions focused. Questions such as "What can you tell me about your best skills?" may or may not produce the information you want. Instead, be focused and ask for specific information. Here is an example: Instead of asking something like...

"Tell me about your experience in training."

you can say something like...

"Think back to when you trained a new employee — tell me exactly what you did to train that employee and bring the person up to the job's performance standards."

Your open-ended questions should be based on the skills definitions you identified after reviewing the technical and performance skills needed to be successful on the job. These are the kinds of questions that will encourage the candidate to give you the information you need to make the right hiring decision.

Keep these three guidelines in mind as you begin developing your interview questions.

Three Guidelines

 Avoid asking questions that can be answered by a single word, usually a simple "yes" or "no".

 Use open-ended questions that ask for specific examples of past job behavior.

 Keep your questions focused.

Take a Moment ...

Listed below are 5 questions. Keeping in mind the three basic guidelines for developing questions, read each question and briefly explain why you think it is or is not a good question to ask in a job interview. Suggested answers appear on page 89.

1. What can you tell me about your last job?

2. Are you married?

3. Have you ever worked on a PC before?

4. Have you ever had to go against your boss? You know, did you ever do something different than what your boss told you to do because you knew your way was better?

5. It's interesting that you want to change careers. Tell me, why do you think you can make the transition into this kind of work?

Four Kinds of Questions

There are four very different kinds of questions you can ask during the course of the job interview. As you begin the interview, you can help put the candidate at ease by asking rapport-building questions. Then, as the candidate becomes more comfortable, you can continue with open-ended questions that invite the candidate to talk about his or her past experiences. Sometimes, in order to get the specific information you need, you will have to use the third kind of question, the probing question. The fourth kind of question will allow you to get a shy candidate to open up. These are non-question questions.

Here's how to prepare these four kinds of questions.

Rapport-Building Questions

Begin your interview by introducing yourself to the candidate. Introductions go more smoothly and lead into more effective interviews when you begin with rapport-building statements and questions. These are intended to...

- Put the candidate at ease.
- Gain the candidate's confidence.
- Show that you and the organization care about the people you are interviewing.
- Demonstrate to the candidate that this is a good place to work.
- Get the candidate to talk about past job behavior.

Remember...your first words to the candidate will set the mood for the rest of the interview. If you begin on a positive note, the candidate will be more likely to open up and talk about past performance.

Here are two examples of **rapport-building statements** and questions:

> *"Pam, thank you for being so prompt. I enjoyed reading through your resume, and I'm looking forward to the time we have together today. May I get you some coffee or a soda?"*

> *"Joe, I'm looking forward to our interview today. I see you listed gulf fishing as one of your hobbies. Tell me more about it. I've seen pictures of it, but have never had the chance to try it myself."*

These kinds of statements and questions encourage the candidate to talk about something he or she is interested in, or that the two of you may share in common. They make it easy for the candidate to start talking, and later, for him or her to provide you with the job-related information you need to make a sound hiring decision.

Using the candidate's name when you first meet helps put the person at ease. Simply showing that you care enough to use the person's name helps communicate that this is a good organization to work for.

3

Take a Moment...

Think in terms of a pending interview you will be conducting. Write out three possible rapport-building statements or questions you can use during the interview:

_____

_____

_____

The time you spend preparing your rapport-building statements and questions will pay big dividends as the candidate relaxes and becomes comfortable talking to you about past job experiences— giving you the information you need to make an informed hiring decision.

Open-Ended Questions

Open-ended questions are questions that cannot be answered by just a few words. Instead, open-ended questions invite the candidate to respond with a good deal of information. The information you're asking for is not opinion or a hypothetical account *("What would you do in a situation where...?")*, but detailed descriptions of how the person handled tasks, responsibilities, and challenges in actual on-the-job situations *("What exactly did you do to correct the problem?")*. Remember, the best predictor of an employee's future performance is past behavior.

Open-ended questions get the candidate to talk about how the person solved a problem, handled a specific responsibility, or carried out a task. Your job is to develop those questions around problems, responsibilities, and tasks that are similar to those encountered on the job for which you're hiring. That's the only way you'll get the kind of specific information you can use to hire the right person for the job you need to fill.

Here are two examples of **open-ended questions** that get at specific instances of past job behavior:

> *"Please think of an instance when you had to discipline an employee. Tell me what you did with that employee to help him or her improve productivity, and why."*

> *"This job involves dealing with difficult customers. Think of a time when you had to deal with a difficult customer and tell me what you did."*

As you prepare your open-ended questions, keep referring to the technical and performance skills needed to be successful in the job. Then make certain that you're asking only those questions that will give you specific information about how the candidate previously performed in similar situations.

"Open-ended questions get the candidate to talk."

Take a Moment...

Think again about the pending job-description example you wrote on page 19. Write five open-ended questions you might use to help you get the information you need to make an informed hiring decision:

_____

_____

_____

_____

_____

Probing Questions

Probing questions are the ones to ask when you need more specific information, or more focused information. Sometimes the candidate...

- Is too nervous to think of the exact detail you want to hear about.
- Doesn't understand the kind of information you want.
- Only partially answers your question.

This is when you need to probe for more specifics. Sometimes you can redirect the candidate by saying something such as...

"Excuse me, John, but let me give you an example of what I'm looking for. You said you enjoyed working with difficult customers. Please take a moment to think about a specific difficult customer you had to deal with. Then tell me exactly how you dealt with that person and how it all turned out."

3

Relate Questions to Skills

Remember, your probing questions also need to be directly related to the technical and performance skills you identified earlier. For example, let's say you are interviewing for a job in which the candidate needs to be able to work as a team member, regardless of how the team may get along all of the time. Your initial question might be something like...

> *"Jennie, tell me about a time when you had to work as part of a team even when the team wasn't getting along all that well, and how you dealt with it."*

Jennie's response might have been too general, something like...

> *"Well, we had two team members who sometimes disagreed on how to get something done. Sometimes when they'd argue, nothing got done."*

An effective **probing question** might be something like...

> *"Jennie, it would help me if you could go into more detail. Think back to a specific time when those two people were arguing, and describe what you did to help the team reach its objectives."*

Gathering Specific Information

By their very nature, probing questions always ask for specific information—information that zeros in on the technical or performance skills you've identified as essential to success on this job.

"Probing questions ask for specific information."

Non-Question Questions

This concept has been around for many years, and used successfully by people in many different situations. Some people use it almost by second nature; others, once they learn of it, are quick to make it their own.

Questions sometimes make people nervous, especially in the setting of a job interview. But you often can make candidates more comfortable responding with the information you need just by asking for it with language that doesn't end in a question mark. Taking the little bit of extra time to rephrase your questions as non-questions can repay big dividends when shy candidates suddenly open up and talk freely about how they get things done.

Here are some examples of **non-question questions:**

Instead of point-blank asking – *"What are your best skills?"* – say something like...

> *"It will help me get to know you better if you can tell me what you believe are your best skills."*

Instead of asking – *"Have you ever had to discipline an employee?"* – try saying something like...

> *"Think back to a time when you had to discipline an employee. Now please briefly set up the situation for me, and then describe exactly what you did."*

Asking non-question questions may not come easy at first. You may need to spend extra time reworking your original questions into non-question form. But once you put the concept into practice, you will find that candidates...

■ Are more relaxed talking with you.

■ Provide more of the kinds of information you need.

■ May even tell you that they've enjoyed the time they spent with you in the interview!

Try using non-question questions. You'll find they're worth every bit of the extra time they may take to prepare!

Allowing for Silence

Occasionally, a candidate will simply have trouble thinking of a specific instance of the kind of behavior you're interested in, and will sit for a moment or two in silence. Don't hesitate to let the person know that silence is okay, and that you don't mind waiting while the person tries to come up with the best example. Remember, a quick response that lacks solid behavioral information does you no good when it's time to make your hiring decision.

"A quick response that lacks solid behavioral information does you no good."

34

Here are two examples of how you can allow for silence in the interview:

"That's all right, Melissa. There's no need to hurry. Take whatever time you need to think of the example you want to tell me about."

"We have lots of time, Carlos. Just let me know when you think of something."

While the candidate thinks and you wait, be sure to sit quietly so you don't disturb the person, or send the subtle message that you are, in fact, in a hurry.

Asking for Contrary Evidence

If ever you begin to realize that you're forming a one-sided impression of the candidate—whether it's all good or all bad—stop and challenge yourself to ask for contrary evidence. For example, if you've been consistently impressed with how the candidate has handled all the difficult situations you've talked about, ask the person to describe a situation in which things just didn't work out as planned:

"Steve, describe a situation in which you had to deal with an irate customer and it didn't work out the way you wanted it to."

Likewise, if you catch yourself forming the impression that the candidate can't do anything right, challenge yourself to ask for contrary evidence here, too. For example, if the candidate has told you about several instances of going against normal procedure when getting things done, ask the person:

"Inga, tell me about a time when you did follow organization procedure, perhaps even when you didn't want to or thought your own ideas would work out better."

"Asking for contrary evidence can prevent you from forming erroneous assumptions or first impressions."

Asking for contrary evidence can prevent you from forming erroneous assumptions or first impressions—and, ultimately, from basing your hiring decisions on them. Of course, there may be times when asking for contrary evidence turns up little or no new information to contradict your earlier impression. In those instances, you'll at least know that you gave a seemingly weak candidate every benefit of the doubt...or that your "perfect" candidate really isn't too good to be true!

Chapter Three Review

Please answer the questions below. Suggested answers appear on page 90.

1. Select the two best interview questions from the following list:
   A) Tell me about your skills.

   B) Can you type?

   C) Have you ever been fired before?

   D) Tell me about a difficult customer you once had to deal with, and how you ended up handling that person.

   E) This position involves supervising four others. Tell me about an employee you may have had to discipline, and describe how you went about it.

   F) Tell me about a problem you've solved before.

2. Indicate whether each of the following statements is **True or False**.

   _____ A) Past behavior has nothing to do with future job performance.

   _____ B) Be sure the interview room is pleasant and arranged so you and the candidate can talk easily.

   _____ C) Probing questions are used to gather more specific information.

   _____ D) How a person has handled a specific situation in the past is a good predictor of the way the person would approach the same kind of situation today.

   _____ E) Effective rapport-building statements and questions at the beginning of the interview help the candidate relax and can make him or her more comfortable sharing information.

3

How Can I Develop Fair and Effective Questions?

Chapter Objectives:

After reading this chapter and completing the interactive exercises, you should be able to:

 Identify and avoid questions that might be construed as discriminatory.

There are questions that can **help you** and questions that can **hinder you** in your search for solid information on which to base a good hiring decision. But there are also questions that can **hurt you**—that may put you and your organization at risk for basing your hiring decisions on what could be considered a discriminatory basis.

This chapter presents questions you can use as models for your own questions, as well as an extensive list of discriminatory questions that you always should avoid.

Discriminatory Questions

Federal legislation states that you cannot base a hiring decision on anything other than **bona fide occupational qualifications** (BFOQ). This means you cannot discriminate against an applicant because of age, sex, marital status, ethnic origin, religious preference, sexual preference, or disabilities.

And this also means that there are certain kinds of questions you simply should not ask during the interview. If you do, the applicant can later claim that he or she was not hired because of something other than a BFOQ. At all costs, you want to avoid any accusation of exercising bias or discrimination in your hiring practices. This involves being aware of related kinds of questions that may be construed by others as intended to gather information that has nothing to do with a person's qualifications.

For example, federal guidelines specifically prohibit you from asking how old a person is or when the person was born. But in an attempt to get around the restriction, some managers have asked, *"When did you graduate from high school?"* This question, however, can be construed as asking for a candidate's age, and therefore being discriminatory in nature, because if you know when a person graduated from high school, you also know, within one or two years, the person's age.

On the following pages are further examples of questions you ***should not*** ask because they are, or appear to be, bias-based.

4

Questions Dealing with Age

How old are you?
When were you born?
When did you graduate from high school?
When did you graduate from college?

Questions Dealing with Marital Status

Are you married?
Do you intend to get married soon?
Do you have children?
Are you a single parent?
Do you practice birth control?
How many people live in your household?
Do you live by yourself?
Can you travel?
Do you have someone who can take care of a sick child?

Questions Dealing with Ethnic Origin

What's your nationality?
Where are your parents from?
What languages do your parents speak?
What other languages do you know?
Are you bilingual?
What's the origin of your name?
What language do you speak at home?

Questions Dealing with Religious Preference

What do you do on Sundays?
What church are you a member of?
Is that a Jewish-sounding name?
Do you sing in the church choir?
Do your children go to Sunday School?
Can you work Friday evenings?
Is there any day in the week you're not able to work?

Are you a member of any religious group?
What religious group are you a member of?
Are you "born again"?

Questions Dealing with Sexual Preference

What's your sexual orientation?
Are you a member of any gay or lesbian groups?
Are you straight?
Do you date members of the opposite or the same sex?

Questions Dealing with Disabilities

What health problems do you have?
Do you have any disabilities?
Are you physically fit and strong?
Is your hearing good?
Can you read small print?
Do you have any back problems?
Have you ever been denied health insurance?
When were you in the hospital the last time?
Do you see a physician on a regular basis?
Do you have large prescription-drug bills?

These are by no means all of the questions you should avoid asking. But these examples should give you an idea of the kinds of questions that might be considered discriminatory. Remember, you cannot ask questions other than those that directly relate to the qualifications needed for the job.

For example, you cannot ask if a person has any disabilities. However, if the job requires the ability to lift up to 50 packages per day, each of which weighs up to 30 pounds, you can ask **each applicant** interviewed:

"Can you lift up to 50 packages per day, each of which may weigh up to 30 pounds?"

You can't ask if a person is married or has children. However, if the job involves spending 30 percent of the employee's time on overnight travel, you can ask **each applicant** something like this:

> *"As you know, the job involves 30 percent overnight travel. Would this be a problem for you?"*

When there are certain valid requirements for the job, you can ask questions that otherwise might be considered discriminatory...if you do it very carefully, and if you **ask each applicant the same question or questions.**

Here's one more example. If the job involves working each Sunday morning, you can ask each applicant something like this:

> *"This job involves working each Sunday morning from 7 a.m. to noon. I just want to let you know this, and to tell you that there are no exceptions, and that it's part of the basic job requirements. Would you have any difficulty meeting this work schedule on a regular basis?"*

If you have any doubt about a specific job qualification that some might consider to be discriminatory in nature, and how to determine if applicants can meet that job qualification, then be certain to seek your organization's legal counsel for their advice.

Chapter Four Review

For each item, select the answer you believe to be correct. Then follow the instructions given in parentheses at the end of the answer you selected.

1. Rapport-building statements and questions...

   ❏ Help put the candidate at ease (go to #5).

   ❏ Keep you from being nervous (go to #7).

2. As I review myself through this Chapter Review, I...

   ❏ Believe I have a good understanding of the kinds of questions I should be asking (go to #20).

   ❏ Believe I need to reread certain sections of this chapter (go to #20).

3. Open-ended questions...

   ❏ Take a lot of time but are worth it (go to #6).

   ❏ Invite the candidate to talk about how he or she gets work done (go to #9).

4. When the candidate does not give you information with enough specificity, you can...

   ❏ Use a probing question or statement (go to #10).

   ❏ Rephrase the question (go to #8).

5. Correct. Rapport-building statements and questions help put the candidate at ease and make it easier for the candidate to give you the information you need. (Continue with #3.)

6. Interviews don't take very long when you ask questions that can be answered in only one word, like "Yes" or "No." The downside is that this kind of question doesn't provide much information. Asking open-ended questions may result in interviews that take longer, but they give you the most useful kind of information. (Continue with #4.)

7. Using rapport-building statements and questions at the beginning of the interview may indeed help you stay calm, but their primary purpose is to put the candidate at ease. If you get nervous conducting interviews, perhaps you could benefit from some additional training in the interviewing processes. (Continue with #3.)

8. Sometimes rephrasing the question will help the candidate better understand what you want to know. But you can also use probing questions to let the candidate know exactly the kind of specifics you want. (Continue with #11.)

9. You're absolutely right! Open-ended questions give the candidate free reign to tell you all they care to about their behavior in past job situations. (Continue with #4.)

10. Congratulations! You're doing well to recognize that probing questions and statements are your best resource for focusing the candidate's responses toward the specific behavior-related information you'll be able to use in making your hiring decision. (Continue with #11.)

11. If ever you realize that you're forming a one-sided impression of the candidate,...

   ❏ Stop and challenge yourself to ask for contrary evidence (go to #12).

   ❏ Be sure to check the candidate's references (go to #15).

12. Great! You're doing well to recall that one-sided impressions can result from assumptions or erroneous first impressions, and cloud your hiring decision. Asking for contrary evidence can help restore the objectivity you need. (Continue with #13.)

13. Federal legislation mandates that you cannot base a hiring decision...

   ❏ On anything other than a BFOQ (go to #16).

   ❏ On anything other than a TQMPC (go to #17).

14. If the job involves extensive overnight travel, you can...

❏ Ask all of your female candidates if it's okay for them to do overnight travel (go to #18)

❏ Ask all candidates if they can comply with the job requirement for overnight travel (go to #19)

15. Yes, you might want to check the candidate's references. However, it's more effective if you ask the candidate for contrary evidence. (Reread the section on Asking for Contrary Evidence starting on page 35, then continue with #13.)

16. You're right. You cannot make a hiring decision on anything other than a bona fide occupational qualification—a BFOQ. (Continue with #14.)

17. Sorry. A TQMPC is just an acronym the author made up, and it has nothing to do with hiring. You can only make hiring decisions based on bona fide occupational qualifications—BFOQs. (Please reread the section on Discriminatory Questions starting on page 39, then continue with #14.)

18. Oops, you really need to reread the section on Discriminatory Questions. To stay in compliance with federal law, you can't ask a question of just a few of your candidates; you must ask it of all candidates. (Continue with #2.)

19. Correct. If the job involves extensive overnight travel, you can ask all candidates if they are able to comply with that particular BFOQ. (Continue with #2.)

20. Thanks for staying with us! Now you're ready for Chapter Five, "How Do I Conduct the Interview?"

4

How Do I Conduct the Interview?

Chapter Objectives:

After reading this chapter and completing the interactive exercises, you should be able to:

 Create the environment for an effective interview.

 Follow the seven steps for conducting the interview:

Step 1: Establish rapport with the candidate.

Step 2: Ask questions about past job performance.

Step 3: Probe to clarify understanding.

Step 4: Seek contrary evidence.

Step 5: Allow the candidate to ask questions.

Step 6: Close the interview.

Step 7: Review your notes and summarize your findings.

Create the Environment for an Effective Interview

Your final task in preparing for the interview is to prepare the interview room. You want the interview room to be comfortable, pleasant, and arranged so you both can talk easily. You'll want to plan so that there will be no outside distractions for either of you. A round table at which both of you can sit probably is the best arrangement. But if you don't have a round table available in the interview room, then seat yourself at a table or desk so that you don't appear intimidating to the candidate.

Arranging the Room

Take a look at your office (or the room in which the interview will be held) and do whatever housekeeping needs to be done. Flat surfaces (desks, tables, and work surfaces) don't necessarily need to be cleared of all books and papers, but they at least should appear neat. Remember that the candidate will form an opinion of the organization based to a great extent on how this room appears. Aim for a pleasing, comfortable appearance.

Choosing Your Attire

You and your attire also are part of the room setting, and you'll want to dress appropriately. But appropriate dress depends on the situation. If you're interviewing for a senior manager, you'll want to dress like a senior manager. On the other hand, just because you happen to be interviewing for a route driver doesn't mean you need to dress like a route driver, unless, of course, that's how you normally would dress for your workday.

5

"Aim for a pleasing, comfortable appearance."

Take a Moment...

Take a moment to look at the room in which you'll be conducting your interviews. Try to be as objective as possible, and ask yourself:

- Does this setting invite the candidate to talk? If not, how can I change it? _____

- Can we both be seated so as to make the interview move smoothly? If not, how can I change it?_____

- Is there anything I could do to make this a better interviewing environment? _____

Seven Steps of the Interview

 Establish Rapport with the Candidate

As you greet the candidate, immediately begin to establish rapport. One of the most effective ways is simply to address the candidate by name. If your organization is like most companies, you'll just use the person's first name. If your organization happens to be more formal, use the person's last name instead, such as Ms. Brown or Mr. Brown.

How do you decide which to use? Ask yourself, *"How do managers address subordinates and peers here at my organization?"* If it's common to use first names, then you should feel comfortable using the candidate's first name during the interview. You'll put the candidate at ease, and at the same time subtly communicate something about the style or culture of the organization.

Creating Rapport

By building rapport and creating a comfortable yet professional atmosphere, you make it easier for the candidate to relax. The candidate will not only react to the organization in a more positive way, but also will give you more complete information. You'll simply have made it easier for the candidate to think of the kinds of specific information about past job behavior that you're looking for.

If you find that you and the candidate share some common experience, such as belonging to the same professional or community organization, talking about it is an effective way to build rapport. You could say something like...

"Janice, I'm very glad to meet you. I've seen you at Toastmasters, and I've been looking forward to our meeting this morning. Tell me, what did you think of Ron's impromptu speech last night?"

Or if you see that you and the candidate have worked at similar jobs in the past, you can begin a short rapport-building discussion like this...

"Joe, I see you started out mixing dye for Ace Textiles. You know, I had a similar job when I began work, too. Tell me, what did you like best about that job?"

Additional examples of rapport-building statements are included in Chapter Three – "How Do I Prepare My Questions?" – starting on page 24.

Taking Notes

After you are seated, take a moment to explain why you will be taking notes during the interview. As you bring out your note pad and **Interview Checklist**, you can say something like...

"Melissa, I'm going to be taking a lot of notes today. It's the best way I know of making sure I don't forget any of the information you give me. This won't bother you, will it?"

If you need extra time to write down some important information, then simply ask the candidate for an extra moment while you catch up. You can say something like...

> *"Melissa, please give me a moment to get all this information down. You've just made an interesting point, and I want to be sure that my notes reflect everything you said."*

Your notes need to summarize the candidate's key responses to your questions, but not necessarily word for word. You simply need to write in enough detail so that, later, you can compare the candidate's responses to your skills inventories. Then you will be able to determine if the candidate demonstrated having the skills you've identified as being necessary for the job.

Here's an example: You ask the candidate to describe how the person handled an angry customer. Your notes might look like this...

> *Has a system for handling irate customers—lets the person talk, doesn't interrupt, and when the customer calms down, begins to ask what the customer would like to have happen. I like this approach!*

What is important is that your notes accurately reflect what the person said, and that they enable you to evaluate whether the candidate has the skills needed to be successful on the job.

2 Ask Questions About Past Job Performance

Since past behavior on the job is the single best predictor of future job performance, your questions should focus on what the candidate did in the past and how the person did it. To encourage the candidate to talk about his or her past experiences in the kind of detail you need, use open-ended questions, which require answers of more than just a few words.

Remember to prepare your questions before the interview. It's always good to begin by reviewing the job description and taking inventory of the skills needed to be successful on the job. Then you can craft your questions to zero in on exactly the information you'll need to make your hiring decision.

To Begin...

You can begin your information-gathering with a general type of question, something like...

"Nancy, why don't you start by telling me about your job at the ABC Organization?"

Your next question can be more specific...

"Nancy, let's get a little more specific. You mentioned that in your job at the ABC Organization, you supervised two others in your office. Tell me about your role as a supervisor."

At the start of most interviews, the information you get from the candidate often will be general in nature. The fact is, most candidates don't take the time to prepare for an interview, and their responses can tend to ramble.

Unfortunately, none of us are born with the natural talent to interview well. It's a learned set of skills, just as conducting an effective interview is a learned set of skills.

5

"Conducting an effective interview is a learned set of skills."

Stay In Control

In order to make the best use of the time you have, you must stay in control of the interview. If the candidate begins to ramble or offer opinions that have nothing to do with your job needs, you can say something like...

> *"Nancy, that's an interesting story, but now I'd like to get back to your job experience. Tell me about...."*

You can be tactful and still maintain control of the interview, directing it toward the information you really need and impressing the candidate with your organization's professionalism at the same time. And remember, as the interview progresses, you can always ask for more detail. If the candidate isn't providing the depth of information you need, use probing questions and statements help the person clarify what he or she is attempting to say.

Take a Moment...

1. Think of the next interview you have to conduct. Now write out two questions you can ask all candidates that will help them talk about their past performance.

   _____

   _____

   _____

   _____

2. The candidate is having a hard time thinking of a specific example to give you. To help the person, you can...

   _____

   _____

   _____

   _____

Probe to Clarify Understanding

When you know how a candidate behaved in past job situations, you can predict how the person will perform in similar situations in the future. Sometimes, however, you'll need to ask probing questions in order to get this kind of specific information. You may even need to give candidates an example of the kind of detail you want. Here's how asking for specifics can follow naturally from an open-ended question...

"Nancy, your comments on how you supervise gave me a lot of good information on the way you help lead others. Now let's get a little more specific. Tell me about a time when you had to ask your people to stay late to complete a project and exactly what you did..."

Here's another way to probe and ask for specifics...

"Nancy, it will help me if you can get more specific. Take whatever time you need to think of a situation in which you had to disagree with your boss about how to handle an employee, and then tell me exactly what you did."

Key phrases you can use to probe for more specific information are:

Tell me about a time...

Describe a situation...

Tell me exactly how you dealt with...

It will help me if you can describe in more detail how you handled...

Think of a specific time you ... and then tell me about what you did.

Remember, you need specific examples of past job behavior so you can evaluate how the person is likely to perform in the new job. Sometimes you have to probe to get the information you want.

Take a Moment...

In response to one of your questions, a candidate tells you that he can deal with irate customers. You want to probe for more detailed, specific information. Write out what you might say.

_____

_____

_____

_____

Allow for Silence

Don't be afraid when the conversation lapses into silence. It can happen. As you ask for specific behavior-related examples, there may be several periods of silence while the candidate recalls just the right example to relate. Silence can work for you, rather than against you.

During the interview, you may need to reassure the candidate that it's acceptable to sit in silence in order to formulate an appropriate response. You might say something like...

It's okay to take your time, Jennie. I know you'll think of something."

"Jim, feel free to take some time to think of the right example. Just let me know when you're ready."

Remember, sometimes our questions pay off only when we wait for the answers.

"Remember, sometimes our questions pay off only when we wait for the answers."

Seek Contrary Evidence

Whenever you feel you're getting a one-sided picture of a candidate, either all good or all bad, it's time to ask for contrary information.

Why?

When an interviewer begins to get a one-sided impression, he or she tends to ask questions that will confirm that impression. This should raise a red flag that the "gut feeling" is still at work. If the interviewer thinks the person is just right and has all the necessary skills, he or she will tend to ask questions that confirm the impression and that continue to put the candidate in a good light. The reverse is also true. When an interviewer thinks a candidate has all the wrong skills or behaviors, he or she tends to ask questions that confirm the impression.

Sometimes all that's needed is to step back, regain perspective, and ask for contrary information. For example, if all your interview questions have focused on situations that turned out well, you should ask a few questions that focus on situations in which things didn't work out well. If you're thinking this candidate truly "walks on water," it's time to ask for contrary information. You can say something like...

> *"Pam, this has been really helpful, and I'm impressed. It would help me now if you could think of a time when working with an angry customer didn't work out, and then tell me what happened."*

Sometimes asking for contrary evidence may change your evaluation of the candidate. Whether contrary evidence confirms or changes your earlier opinion, it will help you make an informed decision based on more extensive information.

5

"Whether contrary evidence confirms or changes your earlier opinion, it will help you make an informed decision."

Allow the Candidate to Ask Questions

Your next step is to ask if the candidate has any questions about the position or the organization. You can say something like...

> *"Felicia, you've given me a lot of good information and I appreciate your ability to stick to the subject. Now it's your turn. Are there questions you would like to ask me about the job or the organization?"*

The kinds of questions you get may vary, depending on how much information the candidate was given prior to or during the interview...and on whether the candidate did any background homework.

Candidates who have a real interest in your position may ask you for more information about...

- What needs to get done on the job.
- What the job's most important task involves.
- How an employee is evaluated.
- The quality of equipment the employee will be working with.
- The first thing the new employee needs to accomplish.

Informed Candidates
Bear in mind that the candidates who traditionally have been the most successful in their jobs were the ones who took time to learn about the organization and the job prior to the interview, and who came prepared for their time to ask questions.

Also understand that a candidate may be more interested in the job's salary and benefits than in accomplishing its tasks if he or she specifically asks about...

- Organization benefits.
- The absenteeism, vacation, and/or sick-leave policies.
- Discipline procedures.
- How to quickly increase the base salary or wage.

Just as you've taken notes on the things the candidate has told you, be sure to take notes on what the person asks you about, too. After the candidate has had an opportunity to ask questions, it's time to bring the interview to a close.

6 Close the Interview

How you close the interview is just as important as how you opened it. You still need to maintain rapport with the candidate, and leave the person with the clear impression that your organization is one of the best they might ever work for.

As you close the interview, you will...

Thank the candidate for his or her interest in the organization and the position. You could say something like...

"Thanks, Duane, for your interest in working at the ABC Organization, and for taking time to meet with me today. It certainly seems that you have made some fine contributions in the past, and are ready for more challenges. Let me tell you what will happen next in our selection process."

Make certain in your closing comments that you don't make any remark that could be construed as an indication that you definitely plan to hire this specific candidate.

Summarize the next action steps. Let each candidate know what your procedure is from this point on, and what your expected time line will be for making a decision. You might say something like...

> *"Duane, we will be interviewing a total of five candidates, and expect to complete interviewing by next Friday. Then we'll conduct a reference check on all candidates, which we plan to finish by the tenth of the month, when we'll make our decision. You can expect to hear from us no later than the 15th of the month."*

Interviewers who share their decision-making plans and time lines with job candidates invariably contribute to their organization's reputation in the marketplace.

Finally ...

One final action you'll want to take is to escort the candidate to the organization entrance or elevator. It takes just a moment, and it adds a touch of professionalism and courtesy that the candidate invariably appreciates and remembers. It's an action that virtually shouts, "Here is a considerate supervisor and a organization that's obviously a good place to work."

Now you have just one more step before the interview process is complete.

Review Your Notes and Summarize Your Findings

The best time to summarize your interview findings is right after the interview. Plan your schedule to allow yourself time after the interview to...

- Review your notes.

- Evaluate the candidate's suitability, comparing the candidate's skills with the previously identified technical and performance skills.

- Summarize your findings in enough detail that, later, you can adequately review all of the candidates at the same time.

For most managers, this is the time to summarize your findings using both the **Interview Checklist** (See the appendix) and your own customized **Candidate Performance Summary Chart,** which is described in detail in the next chapter. Use enough detail to help you recall the strengths and weaknesses of each candidate.

You've done it. You've conducted an interview that has provided all kinds of information highly predictive of the candidate's future performance on the job. Now you're ready to evaluate your candidates and select the best one, based on ***more than a gut feeling.***

"The best time to summarize your interview findings is right after the interview."

5

Chapter Five Review

For each item, select the answer you believe to be correct. Then follow the instructions given in parentheses at the end of the answer you selected.

1. Before the interview, it is important to...

   ❏ Evaluate the interview room, and make any necessary adjustments (go to #9).

   ❏ Be absolutely certain coffee is ready (go to #5).

2. When you begin with rapport-building questions and statements, you...

   ❏ Help the candidate relax and become comfortable (go to #7).

   ❏ Show that you are a person with personality (go to #11).

3. Yes, take a moment to explain why you will be taking notes. It helps put the candidate at ease, and lets the person know that what is said is important to you. (Continue with #15.)

4. Congratulations! You are correct! The single best indicator of future performance is past job behavior. (Continue with #12.)

5. Coffee or a soft drink is always nice, but it's more important first to take a look at your interview room. Does it project the image you want to of the organization, the job, and you as a manager? If not, make the necessary adjustments. (Continue with #10.)

6. It not only is an indicator of future performance, it's the single best indicator of future performance. The majority of your interview will be devoted to talking with the candidate about what he or she did in past jobs. (Continue with #12.)

7. Correct. Rapport-building questions and statements help the candidate relax so he or she can more easily provide the information you need to make an effective decision. (Continue with #8.)

8. At the beginning of the interview, it is important to explain...

   ❑ Why you will be taking notes (go to #3).

   ❑ How you can listen and retain what people say (go to #13).

9. Yes, making certain that the room projects the image you want to convey is very important! You want the interview room to be comfortable, conducive to an effective interview, and reflective of the organization's image. (Continue with #10.)

10. Past performance is...

    ❑ One of three indicators of future performance (go to #6).

    ❑ The single best indicator of future performance (go to #4).

11. Perhaps. But a better reason for establishing rapport at the beginning of the interview is to help put the candidate at ease, so the person will more easily provide the information you need. (Continue with #8.)

12. Sometimes you need to probe for more information. A good probing statement might be...

    "Todd, listen again to my question, and think of a specific example you can tell me about (go to #20)."

    "Todd, let's get more specific. Tell me about a specific time you had to.... (go to #14)."

13. Sorry, but you need to take notes even if you do have a good memory. Taking notes is the best way to recall in detail what each candidate said so that your decision is based not on a gut feeling, but on solid information. (Continue with #15.)

14. Your author prefers this statement to the other example listed. If you would like to review the material on probing questions, refer to Step 3 in this chapter, or Chapter 3. (Continue with #15.)

15. When you find yourself forming a one-sided picture of a candidate, it's time to...

❑ Bring the interview to a close and thank the candidate for his or her time (go to #21).

❑ Ask for contrary information (go to #19).

16. Before the interview is over...

❑ Allow the candidate to ask you questions (go to #18).

❑ Review your notes and **Interview Checklist** (go to #22).

17. As you close the interview...

❑ Thank the candidate (go to #23).

❑ Summarize your next steps in arriving at a decision (go to #24).

18. Yes. Always give the candidate time to ask questions. You can learn a lot from what the candidate asks. (Continue with #17).

19. Yes, this is the time to ask for contrary evidence. And sometimes that contrary information will be just what you're looking for to help you make the best hiring decision. (Continue with #16).

20. Even though you may feel like saying, "Todd, listen to my question again...." there are more effective ways to probe for greater detail. You may want to reread Step 3 in this chapter, Probe to Clarify Understanding, starting on page 53. (Continue with #15).

21. Not hardly! When interviewers find themselves forming a one-sided picture of a candidate, they automatically tend to ask questions that support their assumption. Only by seeking contrary evidence is there an opportunity to regain objectivity and arrive at a balanced evaluation of each candidate. You may want to review Step 4, Seek Contrary Evidence, starting on page 55. (Continue with #16.)

22. Of course, reviewing your notes is important. But you also need to include Step 5, which is allowing the candidate to ask questions. You can gather a lot of useful information from the questions a candidate asks. (Continue with #17).

23. Step 6 is to close the interview by thanking the candidate for his or her interest and time, and summarizing your next action steps. (Continue with #25).

24. Step 6 is to close the interview, by thanking the candidate for his or her interest and time, and summarizing the next action steps. (Continue with #25).

25. Your final step is to review your notes and summarize your findings. ***Good work!***

5

How Do I Evaluate and Select?

Chapter Objectives:

After reading this chapter and completing the interactive exercises, you should be able to:

 Develop a Candidate Performance Summary chart.

☑ Look for possible warning signs.

 Complete your reference checks.

 Review your notes and make your evaluation.

☑ Notify candidates.

You've conducted your interviews using behavior-based questions. You've taken good notes during the interviews on how each candidate responded to your open-ended questions, and on the questions each person asked you. You've probed for specifics. Now it's decision time.

When you have a system for evaluating candidates, you'll take less time to make your decision and you'll do it with more confidence than when you just had your assumptions and intuition to rely on. Your evaluation system is just as important as your interviewing system.

Develop a Candidate Performance Summary Chart

Evaluating candidates after your interviews doesn't have to be tedious or complicated. The Candidate Performance Summary chart (see examples on pages 66 and 67) provides a straightforward way to organize your findings and thoughts about each candidate. With this tool, you can review each candidate fairly and objectively, based on your behavioral interview. Here's how to prepare your chart.

 Review the brief job-description statement you originally wrote, making certain that you've used words that match and describe the skills needed to be successful on the job.

 Review the primary technical skills you've identified as essential for the person to do the job, and list them on your technical skills performance summary chart. See page 66 for an example.

 Review the primary performance skills you've identified as essential for the person to do the job. An example of a complete chart is shown on page 67.

With your charts completed, you're ready to review your notes from each candidate's interview and summarize your findings. After you've gained some experience completing these Candidate Performance Summary charts, you may want to set up your charts before your round of interviews, and fill in your findings about each candidate when you review your notes after each interview.

6

Candidate Performance Summary

Technical Skills

Position ___Customer Service Supv.___ **Date** _____ **Interviewer** ___Terri___

Job Candidate	PC Experience	Lotus 1-2-3	Simplex Phone System	Word for Windows	Experience with databases
Ann	Yes at home	No	No experience but aware of it	Yes	Limited
Ben	Yes	Yes	Used ABC system	Yes	No
Felicia	Yes	Yes	Recommended system in last position	Also WordPerfect	Yes - MS Excell
Melissa	Yes at home	Yes	Yes	Yes	Familiar w/ Q&A and DBase III

Candidate Performance Summary

Performance Skills

Position ___Customer Service Supv.___ Date _____ Interviewer ___Terri___

Job Candidate	Supervise 5 Employees	Schedule Work	Train New Employees	Interact with Other Depts.	Prepare Budget	Assist Customers	Prepare Reports	Member of Supv. Team	Other
Ann	Supv 3	Yes	Trained 1	No	For supplies	Very good	Yes	Yes active	Enjoys customer service
Ben	Supv 2	Yes	Trained several - high turnover	Dealt with shipping and accounting	Didn't prepare - but monitored	Very good	OK	Yes - limited involvement	Wants more responsibility
Felicia	No previoussu	Scheduled rooms & cars	Active ASTD	No - but lots of community work	ASTD budget $35,000	Very good	Yes	No - but member of ASTD board	Wants more respons. - ready for it
Melissa	Supv 3	Yes	Trained several ASTD	Yes - chaired inter-dept team	Yes - $100,000	Very good	Yes	Yes - chaired team for 1 year	Eager - wants more responsibility

Look for Possible Warning Signs

As you review your summary charts, you may realize that you've gathered some items of information about one or more candidates that would cause you to hesitate before making an offer to the person. Some candidates will give you warning signs that they may, in fact, not be right for your organization. These tip-offs can include...

- The candidate once quit a job without giving adequate notice.

- The candidate arrived late for your interview and offered no explanation.

- You detect the smell of alcohol on the candidate.

- The candidate demands that you match an offer by his or her current employer.

- You're unable to verify any of the candidate's references.

Please understand that none of these examples on its own necessarily warrants a "no-hire" decision. However, whenever you come across one of them, it's time to stop and review your evaluation of the candidate.

Take a Moment...

Identify three other managers at your organization who have good track records for hiring new employees. Ask each of them to review the above list of warning signs, and ask them if they've encountered additional indicators that a candidate may not be right for a position with the organization. Incorporate their suggestions into your own list of possible warning signs.

Complete Your Reference Checks

Companies are increasingly adopting the policy of not releasing information about former employees other than dates of employment and, in some instances, job titles. Even so, checking references can be worth the time and effort.

Questions to Ask

Questions you can ask references that may help you make your hiring decision are:

- How long have you known this person, and how did you become acquainted?

- Have you worked with this person before? Where? In what context?

- What are this person's strengths?

- What is one skill that this person needs to work on?

- Why would you hire this person? (Or, if you're speaking with a representative of a former employer, "Is this person eligible for rehire?")

Checking references is one more way to ensure that you base your hiring decision on more than a gut feeling.

Review Your Notes and Make Your Evaluation

Your summary chart has been prepared, you've reviewed your notes for any possible warning signs, and you've checked all candidate references. Now is when your interview notes really prove their worth, because if they aren't sufficiently detailed, it will be difficult to recall if a candidate gave you the kind of behavior-related information you now need.

Review your notes from each interview, and compare them with each other and with the technical and performance skills you've listed on your summary charts. See the examples shown on page 66 and 67 on how to complete the summary chart.

Take a Moment...

Review the two sample Candidate Performance Summary charts on pages 66 and 67. Which of these candidates—Ann, Ben, Felicia, or Melissa—would you hire? Why? Make your decision and write the name of your top candidate in the space below. Then compare your selection with the author's choice, which is explained on page 90.

My top candidate is:_____

My reasons for hiring this candidate are:

_____

_____

_____

_____

_____

_____

_____

_____

Notify Candidates

Your final task in the hiring process is to notify all candidates of your hiring decision. Your first communication, usually a phone call, will, of course, be to the successful candidate as you—or someone from your organization's personnel department—make the job offer. For exempt positions, this usually involves an offer over the phone followed the same day by a letter detailing the offer. More and more, supervisory, managerial, and executive candidates also expect to receive a letter outlining the offer and detailing the various forms of compensation.

Wait until your first choice says "Yes" before notifying the other candidates. That way, if your first choice declines the offer, you still can contact one of the other candidates if any of them have the skills needed to be successful in the job.

Give the candidate time to consider the offer before responding with their answer. How much time? Up to several days is fairly standard, depending on the level and location of the position. If you need the position filled quickly, you can tell the finalist that you need to confirm the position as soon as possible.

Offers to successful candidates for non-exempt positions also tend to be handled over the phone. However, you enhance your organization's reputation in the marketplace if you also send a confirmation letter summarizing the job, start date, and compensation.

But wait! You're still not done!

- What about those other candidates you talked with?
- What about individuals who applied for the position but were not interviewed?
- What about maintaining your organization's reputation in the marketplace?

> **"Give the candidate time to consider the offer before responding with their answer."**

6

Your hiring procedure needs to include a notification step for these people, too, or you run the risk of hurting your organization's reputation as a good place to work.

Notifying Candidates Not Chosen

The quickest way to accomplish these notifications is to send an effective letter to your applicants. The letter needs to be well-written, professional in appearance, and above all, personal! Fill-in-the-blank form letters and tersely worded postcards definitely have no place here. Put yourself in the shoes of the person who will receive your letter, and ask yourself, *"Did it make me feel I was treated courteously, professionally, and as an individual?"*

On the following pages are sample letters for both interviewed and non-interviewed applicants.

Sample notification letter to non-interviewed applicants:

Date

John Doe
Home Address
City/State/Zip Code

Dear John Doe:

Thank you for your interest in the position of ... with the ABC Organization. We had many applications, and it was not easy to decide whom we would interview.

Though it appeared from your application that you had some of the skills we need for the position, there were others who had more of the skills it will take to be successful in that job.

We will keep your resume on file for the next year [or however you handle applicant resumes]. If there are other positions here at the ABC Organization for which you believe you have the necessary qualification, please contact us.

Thank you for your interest in our organization. I wish you well in your search for a position in which you can be successful.

Sincerely,

Manager

6

Sample notification letter to interviewed candidates who did not receive the offer:

Date

John Doe
Home Address
City/State/Zip Code

Dear John Doe:

Thank you for your interest in the position of ... at the ABC Organization. We appreciate your interest in being part of our employee team, as well as the time you spent talking with us.

Our offer has been accepted by another candidate. Though you have many of the skills we believe are important to be successful in this position, we found the other candidate to have even more of the skills and experience we need at this time.

We will keep your application on file for the next year, and will contact you if we have an opening that calls for a person with your skills and experience. Likewise, please don't hesitate to contact us regarding any future openings you feel match your skills and experience.

Again, thank you for your interest in the ABC Organization. We all wish you well in your pursuit of a position that makes full use of your skills, abilities, and experience.

Sincerely,

Manager

Chapter Six Review

Fill in the blanks for each of the following statements. Suggested answers appear on page 90 and 91.

1. When you review your notes from each candidate's interview, you should compare your _____ with the information provided by the candidate.

2. Candidate Performance Summary charts should list both the job's _____ and _____ skills.

3. You go beyond just a gut feeling when you base your hiring decision on the candidate's _____.

4. Two warning signs that a candidate may not be right for your position include _____ and _____.

5. One way for a organization to enhance its reputation as a good place to work is to _____.

CHAPTER SEVEN

How Do I Handle Difficult Interviewing Situations?

Chapter Objectives:

After reading this chapter and completing the interactive exercises, you should be able to deal with most **"What if...?"** situations, including:

 What if the candidate is late?

 What if the candidate won't talk?

 What if the candidate won't stop talking?

 What if the candidate can't provide specific examples?

 What if the candidate has misrepresented himself or herself?

 What if the candidate is totally unqualified?

Even with the best preparation, you still may encounter situations that go beyond normal. Maybe a candidate just can't think of anything to say, or talks too much, or even has misrepresented his or her qualifications. This chapter presents six "What if...?" situations to help you more effectively deal with these extraordinary circumstances.

What If the Candidate Is Late?

Even though most candidates will arrive at least 10 minutes early for a job interview, some may show up late. Events beyond their control do take place, and though the candidate tries, he or she just may not be able to get there on time. The person may keep you waiting 10 minutes, or sometimes even longer.

The responsible candidate will call, if possible, to advise you that he or she will be late. If the candidate can't make the appointment at all, the responsible person will call prior to the scheduled time. You then can arrange another time for the interview to take place.

What if the candidate is 15 minutes late and hasn't called? That fact becomes part of your information about the person's performance. You'll naturally want to know why the candidate was late and if the person was somehow unable to call, and provide time for an explanation. Remember, sometimes you need to seek contrary evidence; during the interview, you may decide to ask for more detail about the person's record of being on time.

You Should ...

If the candidate is late, don't jump to conclusions either way. You need more information before you decide if the late arrival is an important behavioral factor.

7

What If the Candidate Won't Talk?

There are people who become so nervous during an interview that they literally can't think of what to say. So they sit and say nothing. What do you do?

Remember that part of your goal during the interview process is to help the organization maintain or even enhance its image as a good place to work. This means exercising tact and professionalism, and being careful not to appear impatient or to make light of the situation. Instead, treat the candidate with regard and as much empathy as you can.

You can say something like...

> *"Roger, that's okay. Take your time thinking about what you want to say. When you're ready, just go ahead and tell me about your last job. Would you like a cup of coffee?"*

If, for whatever reason, the candidate just isn't able to continue, ask if the person would like to reschedule the interview for another mutually convenient time.

What If the Candidate Won't Stop Talking?

A more common problem is the candidate who won't stop talking. You ask a question and the person answers, and answers, and answers.

You need to help these talkers maintain focus with their responses. You could wait for the person to pause, but sometimes you'll simply need to interrupt.

You can say something like...

> *"Sara, that's an interesting story, but we need to stay focused on how your experience and skills apply to the job needs here at the ABC Organization. Let me rephrase my question so you can give me the kind of specific information."*

If the person continues to ramble, be courteous but firm. And remember that what you say—and how you say it—reflects on your organization's image as a great place to work.

As a friend once said, *"Some people are reinforced by the sound of their own voice."* Nothing you can say may get this kind of person to refrain from rambling. So when you find yourself in this kind of situation, make a note of it and bring the interview to a close.

What If the Candidate Can't Provide Specific Examples?

Sometimes in their nervousness during the interview, a candidate just won't be able to recall the kind of specific behavior-based examples you're asking for. In this situation, you can...

- Coach the candidate, by giving an example of the depth of information you're looking for.
- Refer to the person's resume, and ask for detailed information about a specific item listed there.
- Let the person talk in generalities for a brief time, then try asking for in-depth specifics once again.

You Should...

If the candidate still can't provide you with specific examples, you need to make a decision. Is the person so nervous that he or she just can't think of specifics? Or are there simply no specifics to talk about. In other words, has the person misrepresented himself or herself? Your thoughts should be placed in your notes and referred to in your final decision.

7

What If the Candidate Has Misrepresented Himself or Herself?

If you begin to suspect that the candidate has misrepresented himself or herself at some point during the application and screening process, you must quickly decide...

■ Did the person not fully understand the position and its requisite skills and experience, and you are, in fact, both talking about two different jobs?

■ Did the person get overly ambitious in describing his or her skills and experience?

■ Is the person someone who you suspect regularly misrepresents his or her qualifications during a job search?

Using probing questions, you can ask for information to help you make your decision about which of these possible scenarios applies to this candidate. Your next steps will depend on the decision you make.

If you believe the person **didn't fully understand the position** announcement, you can say something like...

"Steve, it seems that you and I are talking about two different kinds of jobs. From your descriptions of your past performance, it just doesn't seem to me that what you've listed on your resume really applies to this particular position. Perhaps we need to close this interview, and then I can tell you how to apply for other positions here at the ABC Organization."

If you believe the candidate became **overly zealous in describing himself or herself**, you might say something like...

"Steve, I'm wondering if you might have been overly ambitious in describing some of your past responsibilities and accomplishments. The skills and experience you've told me about just aren't what we need for this specific position. If you'd like, I can tell you how you can apply for other positions here at the ABC Organization."

If, on the other hand, you strongly suspect that this person **routinely and deliberately misrepresents qualification** in hiring situations, you should say something like...

"Steve, whenever I've asked you for specifics, it's been clear from your answers that your experiences and skills aren't what we need for this position. I appreciate your interest, but I'm afraid it is not a good use of time for either of us to continue with this interview."

What If the Candidate Is Totally Unqualified?

From time to time and for a variety of reasons, you may get all the way to the interview stage with a candidate who is totally unqualified for your job. Remembering the need to maintain your organization's good reputation, you can say something like...

"Karen, it seems fairly clear that your skills and experiences are not what we need in the person who fills this position. Here at the ABC Organization, we're careful to match employee skills with those needed for specific jobs. And though you have some fine qualities, your skills don't match this job's particular set of needs. I appreciate the time you've spent talking with us, and if you're interested, I'll be glad to tell you how to apply for other positions here."

It is important that you...

- Are direct in stating that the person does not have the needed skills and experiences.
- Are courteous in what you say.
- Refrain from saying anything that could be taken as an indication that you based your decision on anything other than a BFOQ.

Chapter Seven Review

Please answer the questions below. Suggested answers appear on page 91.

1. The candidate calls to report that he is having car trouble and will be 15 minutes late. He finally arrives, close to 45 minutes late. How would you react?

   _____

   _____

2. When you encounter a candidate who rambles and won't stop or who isn't truly qualified, you must remember...

   A) Not to waste organization time.

   B) That part of your role is to enhance the organization's positive image.

   C) That sometimes people are more than they appear, and since your instincts told you this was a viable candidate, you should seek contrary evidence to find out what the person can really accomplish for your organization.

3. **True or False:** Sometimes you have to interrupt a candidate and remind him or her of the need to stay on the subject without rambling.

4. If you suspect that the candidate has misrepresented himself or herself, you need to decide if the person...

   A) Didn't fully understand the position announcement.

   B) Was overly ambitious in describing past experiences and accomplishments.

   C) Blatantly misrepresented himself or herself.

   D) All of the above scenarios are correct.

7

CHAPTER EIGHT

How Do I Implement Behavior-Based Interviewing?

Chapter Objectives:

After reading this chapter and completing the interactive exercises, you should be able to:

- ☑ Assess your readiness to implement behavior-based interviewing.

- ☑ Identify what you need to do to implement behavior-based interviewing.

- ☑ Develop a *Plan for Action*.

> **"Your task in the hiring interview is to gather the kinds of information that will enable you to hire people who will be successful in their jobs!"**

By now you no doubt understand that the single best predictor of future job performance is past job behavior. You also realize that your task in the hiring interview is to gather the kinds of information that will enable you to hire people who will be successful in their jobs!

Now the question is, are you ready?

Personal Assessment

The key principles of *Interviewing: More Than a Gut Feeling* are summarized below. Take time now to review each statement and honestly evaluate your understanding of it, or your preparedness to implement it:

Poor   *Excellent*

1 2 3 4 5 6 7   I understand and can explain to others how past job behavior is the single best predictor of future job performance.

1 2 3 4 5 6 7   I understand and can explain to others how making decisions based on more than a gut feeling can help reduce employee turnover and increase compliance with federal hiring guidelines.

1 2 3 4 5 6 7   I believe that by following a hiring procedure that helps me make decisions based on *more than a gut feeling*, my organization's reputation in the marketplace can be enhanced.

1 2 3 4 5 6 7   I can review a position description and identify and describe the technical skills needed to be successful in that job.

1 2 3 4 5 6 7   I can review a position description and identify and describe the performance skills needed to be successful in that job.

1 2 3 4 5 6 7   I can prepare appropriate rapport-building questions and statements.

Poor   *Excellent*

1 2 3 4 5 6 7   I can prepare appropriate open-ended questions.

1 2 3 4 5 6 7   I understand how to use probing questions and statements to gather specific information.

1 2 3 4 5 6 7   I understand and can describe to others each of the seven steps for conducting the interview.

1 2 3 4 5 6 7   I believe I can deal with a variety of "What if...?" situations.

1 2 3 4 5 6 7   I can develop and use the Candidate Performance Summary charts to help me make my hiring decision.

1 2 3 4 5 6 7   I am aware of certain warning signs that can indicate that a particular candidate may not be right for the job.

1 2 3 4 5 6 7   I can draft personal, professional letters to notify applicants and interview candidates of my final hiring decision.

1 2 3 4 5 6 7   I can effectively notify the successful candidate, make the job offer, and prepare a letter summarizing the job offer.

1 2 3 4 5 6 7   I believe I am ready to implement a behavior-based hiring procedure.

After you have completed this self-evaluation, review your results. Make the decision to develop a plan that will move any 1-2-3 ratings into the 6-7 range. You need to be ready in each category before you can successfully implement behavior-based interviewing.

Your Plan for Action

Interviewing: More Than a Gut Feeling has provided you with the essential resources and tools to put behavior-based interviewing into practice. The book began by introducing the concept that the best predictor of future job performance is past job behavior, and then summarizing the key reasons it's important to practice effective hiring procedures.

The book has introduced you to several tools that make it easy to implement those procedures.

Now it's time to use these tools to increase your effectiveness in interviewing and making hiring decisions. What does it take to implement behavior-based interviewing? Just time, practice, and a willingness to make it work. Here are the major resources you'll need:

- Commitment from key decision-makers to implement hiring procedures based on *more than a gut feeling*.

- Identification of the technical skills needed to be successful in each specific job.

- Identification of the performance skills needed to be successful in each specific job.

- Time after each interview to review notes, compare the candidate's skills with required skills inventories, and complete the Candidate Performance Summary charts.

- Resources to adequately respond to each applicant, so your organization earns an enviable reputation in the marketplace.

8

You can implement behavior-based interviewing all by yourself, or as part of a department-wide effort. And though it will take more time, you can be the catalyst to help its adoption organization-wide.

Just think...

- You can improve your effectiveness in making hiring decisions.
- You can identify and place people in jobs where they will be most successful.
- You can make it happen!

What does it take? The information provided in this book can help you make your hiring decisions based on solid information...with ***more than just a gut feeling.***

Answers to Exercises

Chapter One

Chapter Review (from page 15)

Statements 2 and 5 are False. The rest are True.

Chapter Two

Chapter Review (from page 23)

1. Technical Skills include:
    *   COBOL
    *   BASIC
    *   Lotus 1-2-3
    *   Q&A
    *   Networked PC's

    Performance Skills include:
    *   Supervising the work of five others
    *   Scheduling the work of the five programmers
    *   Interacting with three departments
    *   Helping end-users identify real needs
    *   Helping programmers understand the needs of end-users
    *   Presenting information to end user in the three departments
    *   Solving problems when they occur
    *   Assigning priority to projects
    *   Explaining project priority to end-users
    *   Remaining organized yet flexible enough to help solve immediate problems

Chapter Three

Take A Moment (from page 27)

The author nominates questions 4 and 5 as the ones likely to give you the most specific information about past job behavior. One question—number 2—isn't just poor, it's illegal!

Chapter Review (from page 37)

1. The two best questions are items D and E.

   D) Tell me about a difficult customer you once had to deal with, and how you ended up handling that person.

   E) This position involves supervising four others. Tell me about an employee you may have had to discipline, and describe how you went about it.

2. Statement A is False. The rest are True.

Chapter Six

Take a Moment... (from page 70)

Author's rationale: My choice is Melissa, though it was a close decision. All of the candidates have PC experience, as well as experience with Microsoft Word for Windows. Ann has no direct experience with the Simplex Phone System, and Felicia is thoroughly familiar with it. On the "plus" side, both Felicia and Melissa have database experience. When I factored in technical skills, I narrowed the field to Felicia and Melissa.

The candidates show much similarity in their performance skills. All have supervised others (with the exception of Felicia), all have scheduling experience, and all have trained at least one new employee. However, here Melissa stands out because of her experience interacting with other departments, and her past work with budgets. All were evaluated "very good" on helping customers, and met the criteria in their ability to prepare reports. But Melissa again emerged as the top candidate with supervisory-team experience, having chaired a supervisory team within a work unit for one year. All candidates demonstrated that they either enjoyed customer service or were ready for more customer-service responsibility. Based on all these criteria, my first offer goes to Melissa.

Chapter Review (from page 75)

1. When you review your notes from each candidate's interview, you should compare your skills definitions or skills inventories with the information provided by the candidate.

2. The Candidate Performance Summary charts should list both the job's technical and performance skills.

3. You go beyond just a gut feeling when you base your hiring decision on the candidate's past performance.

4. Some possible warning signs that a candidate may not be right for your position include: The candidate quit a job without providing adequate notice, accepts salary terms and then tries to increase them, arrives late for your interview with no explanation, smells of alcohol, demands that you match another offer, can't supply verifiable references, reveals confidential information, can't provide specific behavioral examples to back up general statements, or bad-mouths a previous employer.

5. One way for a company to enhance its reputation as a good place to work is to notify all applicants with a personal, professional letter.

Chapter Seven

Chapter Review (from page 83)

1. Give the candidate an opportunity to explain why he was late. If no explanation is offered, you might decide to probe for more information before deciding if this is relevant behavioral information.

2. Definitely, B. In fact, you should keep your company's image and its reputation in the marketplace uppermost in mind throughout the interview process.

3. True

4. D is the correct choice, since all three of the previous scenarios are possibilities.

Interview Checklist

This checklist has been designed to help you think through the issues and logistics for interviewing. Though each item may not apply to every situation, it is important that you respond to each line. When you have provided the information called for, check the box for each section so that you know it has been considered and the appropriate planning is done. Your planning is not completed until all items have been checked.

C O N F I D E N T I A L

_____

For use by

Supervisor/Manager

Interview Checklist

This **Interview Checklist** has been designed to help you plan for each candidate interview for a specific position. Respond to each item with the requested information, and then check-mark it when your plans are complete.

Candidate: _____

Date of Interview: _____ Position: _____

Interview to Be Conducted by: _____

Manager: _____

☐ 1. Interview scheduled for:

   Date: _____ Time: _____ Location: _____

☐ 2. Brief description of position: _____

   _____

   _____

☐ 3. Position specifics:

   Title: _____ Salary: _____

   Grade/Level: _____ Department: _____ Start Date: _____

   Other: _____

   _____

☐ 4. Notes for rapport-building statements/questions: _____

   _____

   _____

❑ 5. Questions about technical skills to be asked of all candidates:_____

_____

_____

❑ 6. Questions about performance skills to be asked of all candidates: _____

_____

_____

❑ 7. Additional questions (if needed): _____

_____

_____

❑ 8. Immediately after the interview, review your notes about the interviewee's technical
and performance skills, and compare them with those needed to be successful on the
job. Summarize your findings in the space below: _____

_____

_____

_____

❑ 9. Further action: _____

_____

❑ Additional interview: Recommended?   ❑ Yes   ❑ No

Letter to be sent:_____

Other:_____

_____

Candidate Performance Summary

Position: _____ **Date:** _____ **Interviewer:** _____

Job Candidate					

Additional Resources
from American Media Incorporated

Other AMI How-to Series Books
Assertiveness Skills
Customer Service Excellence
I Have To Fire Someone!
Investing Time for Maximum Return
Making Meetings Work
Managing Conflict at Work
Managing Stress
Self-Esteem: The Power to Be Your Best
Ten Tools for Quality
The Human Touch Performance Appraisal
The New Supervisor: Skills for Success

Videos Pertaining to the Subject of Interviewing
Communication Connection
Coping with Difficult People
Constructive Communication! How to Give It and How to Take It
Impressions Count and So Do You!
Relationship Strategies
Solving Conflict
Stress: You're in Control
Take Time To Listen
Team Player
That's Not my Problem
Together We Can!
Why Didn't I Think of That?

Other Videos Available On These Subjects
*Americans with Disabilities Act • AIDS Awareness • Banking • Business Writing •
Change • Communication • Computer PC Training • Conflict Resolution •
Creative Problem Solving • Cultural Diversity • Customer Service • Empowerment •
Ethics • Family and Medical Leave Act • Healthcare Employee Training •
Healthcare Safety • Icebreaker • Interviewing • Listening Skills • Motivation •
Outplacement • Paradigms • Performance Appraisal • Professional Image • Quality •
Retail • Safety • Sales Training • Sexual Harassment • Stress • Substance Abuse •
Supervision • Teamwork • Telephone Skills • Time Management • And Many More!*

**To order additional American Media Incorporated resources,
call your Training Consultant at:
(800) 262-2557**